DOMINANTPENTATONIC SCALEGUITARSOLOING

Discover The Secret Weapon For Advanced Modern Soloing On Dominant Chords

SHAUN**BAXTER**

FUNDAMENTAL**CHANGES**

Dominant Pentatonic Scale Guitar Soloing

Discover The Secret Weapon For Advanced Modern Soloing On Dominant Chords

ISBN: 978-1-78933-437-1

Published by **www.fundamental-changes.com**

Copyright © 2024 Shaun Baxter

Edited by Joseph Alexander

www.fundamental-changes.com

For over 350 free guitar lessons with videos check out:

www.fundamental-changes.com

Join our free Facebook Community of Cool Musicians

www.facebook.com/groups/fundamentalguitar

Cover Image Copyright: Shaun Baxter

All audio for Chapters 1, 6, 7 and 8 recorded and mixed at Brakenhurst Studio by Shaun Baxter.

All audio for Chapters 2, 3, 4, 5 and 9 recorded and mixed at W.M. Studios by Phil Hilborne.

All transcriptions by Shaun Baxter.

Contents

About the Author

Shaun Baxter is a world-renowned guitar player and the UK's most experienced and respected rock guitar teacher.

He was a founder member of The Guitar Institute in London in 1986 (which was partnered with the London College of Music and became the biggest trade-school for guitar in Europe) where he taught every week for over twenty years. He went on to be Head of Guitar at Guitar-X in London before, in 2003, becoming an owner and the Academic Director of The Academy of Music and Sound (AMS), a national network of musical schools, opening centres all over the UK. At one point, via their various apprenticeship schemes, AMS were the biggest employer in the Scottish music industry and their alumni includes Lewis Capaldi.

Shaun composed the world's first Grade 8 Guitar syllabus for Trinity College, wrote the UK's National Operational Standards (NOS) for music performance, and contributed to magazines such as *The Guitar Magazine*, *Guitar World*, *Metal Hammer* and *Guitar Techniques* (for whom he wrote a popular and influential monthly column for 27 years).

Through his teaching, Shaun helped to pioneer popular music education in the UK and taught many high profile guitarists such as Rick Graham, Andy James, Jon Gomm and Justin Sandercoe, as well as many others who have found fame with artists such as Public Image Ltd, Asia, Craig David, Moby, Wynton Marsalis, Haken, Martin Taylor, Steve Hackett, Rick Wakeman, Mike Oldfield, The Art of Noise, Leo Sayer, Pet Shop Boys, Roger Waters and Queen.

During the '90s, he was a member of the Composition Department at the London College of Music and also lectured at Brunel University, Leeds College of Music, University of West London, Bath Spa University, Coventry University and Rostock University of Music and Drama in Germany.

In 1993, Shaun recorded his ground-breaking *Jazz Metal* solo album.

He has performed with players such as Uli Jon Roth (Scorpions), Neil Murray (Whitesnake, Black Sabbath), and Ron "Bumblefoot" Thal (Guns & Roses), and also toured the world and/or recorded with artists such as Princess, John Sloman (Gary Moore/Uriah Heep), Todd Rundgren and Carl Palmer of Emerson Lake and Palmer.

"He is one of the greatest musicians I have played with." (Carl Palmer, legendary progressive rock drummer).

As an artist, he has been an official endorsee of Marshall Amplification, Cornford Amplification, Fender Guitars, Patrick Eggle Guitars, Line 6 effects, Two-Note Audio Engineering, and Picato Strings.

Finally, Shaun was one of only eight heavy metal guitar players (along with Edward Van Halen, Joe Satriani, Steve Vai, Yngwie Malmsteen, Nuno Bettencourt, Michael Schenker and Paul Gilbert) featured in the world's biggest-selling music book, *Guitar: A Complete Guide for the Player* (2002).

Shaun appeared in a list of "the top 50 rock guitar players since the 1980s" in *Guitarist* magazine and was also included in *The Guitarist's Book of Guitarist Players* (1994) which details "the world's most influential guitarists and bass players". His album, *Jazz Metal* topped its 50 recommended fusion guitar recordings.

Shaun is the bestselling author of *Chromatic Lead Guitar Techniques*, published by Fundamental Changes.

Introduction

The Dominant Pentatonic scale is an incredibly effective way to play over static dominant seventh chords. But what is the Dominant Pentatonic and where does it come from?

In Western music, Mixolydian is the seven-note scale most often used to play over dominant 7 chords, because it is effectively a major scale with a flattened seventh degree. This set of tones allows us to outline the 1, 3, 5 and b7 of a dominant chord and then add rich intervals around them (the 2nd, 4th and 6th).

If we were playing over an A7 chord, we would use the A Mixolydian scale which has the notes: A, B, C#, D, E, F#, G.

You probably already know that it is common to extract a five-note structure from Mixolydian called the Major Pentatonic scale. A Major Pentatonic uses five notes from A Mixolydian:

A Major Pentatonic Scale	A	B	C#	E	F#
Formula	1	2	3	5	6

Although this scale is used extensively in Soul, R&B and Country music, it doesn't include the b7 needed to outline a dominant 7 chord, and many musicians consider the 6th to sound too undefined in this setting. Instead, they prefer to use the lesser-known Dominant Pentatonic – a major pentatonic scale where the b7 replaces the 6th.

A Dominant Pentatonic	A	B	C#	E	G
Formula	1	2	3	5	b7

If we slightly rearrange these notes, we can also view this scale as spelling a dominant 9 arpeggio, compressed into the space of one octave.

A Dominant 9 Arpeggio	A	C#	E	G	B
Formula	1	3	5	b7	9

Play an A9 chord and you will see that all five notes are contained in the A Dominant Pentatonic scale.

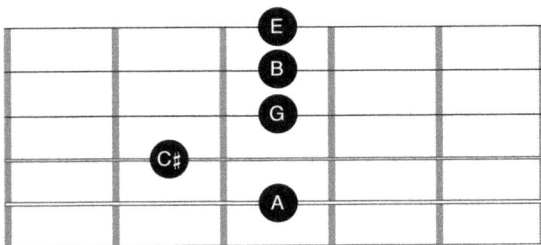

If you need to solo over a series of dominant 7 chords, you'll find that playing the Dominant Pentatonic scale from the root of each one will bring out the flavour of the chords much more successfully than any other pentatonic scale.

If you use the Dominant Pentatonic in a blues setting, by playing the scale from the root of each dominant 7 chord (e.g., A7, D7 and E7) you will be able to convey the sound of the chord progression to the listener, even when playing unaccompanied.

In this book, we're going to look at various ways of using this scale, and exploit its relationship with its parent Mixolydian scale to create harmonically articulate lines and solos over dominant 7 chords.

The diagrams below show the five CAGED shapes of the A Mixolydian scale across the neck, and highlight the A Dominant Pentatonic scale contained within using black notes. Looking at the patterns you can see that the Dominant Pentatonic shape is created by omitting the 4th and 6th intervals (white notes) from each shape.

Although we'll apply the Dominant Pentatonic scale in a whole manner of different ways, these shapes will serve as our visual reference points throughout.

Shape 1

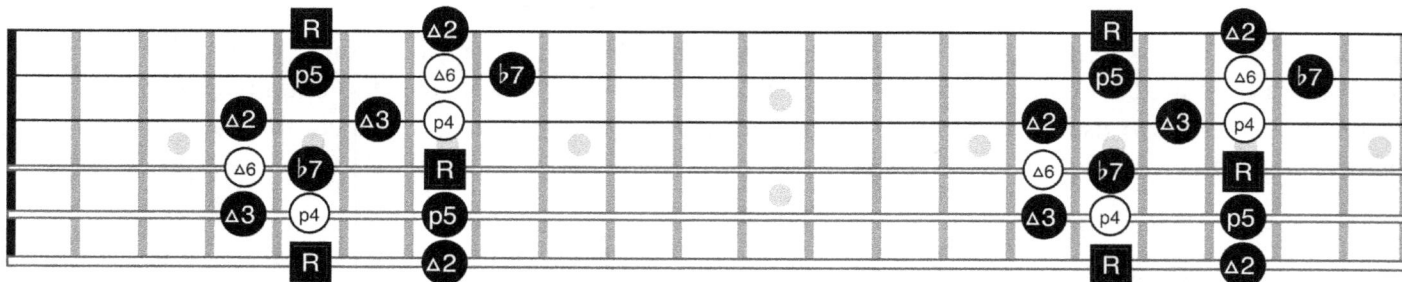

Shape 2

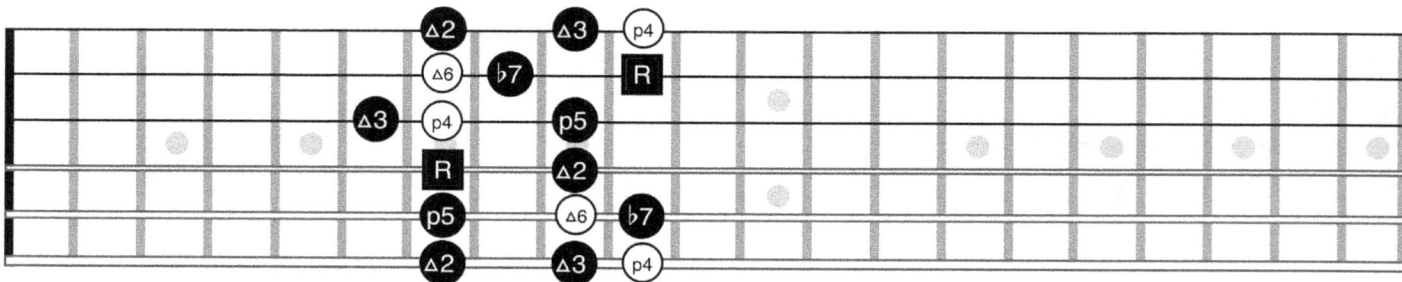

Shape 3

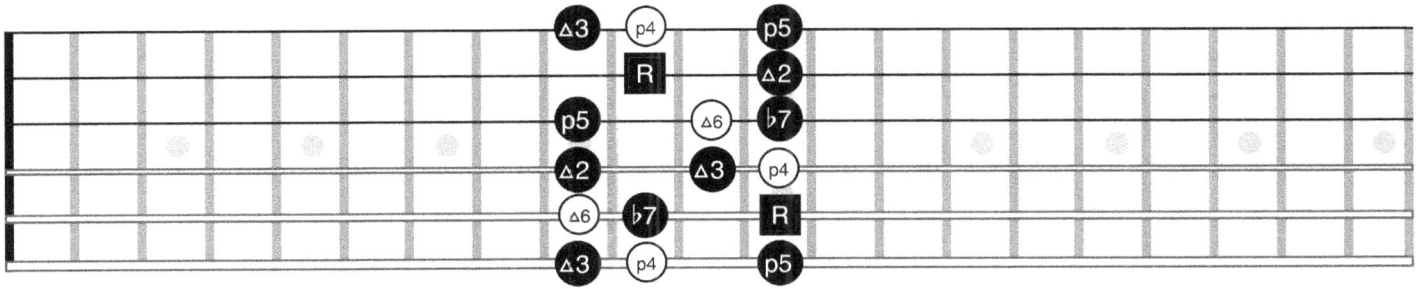

Shape 4

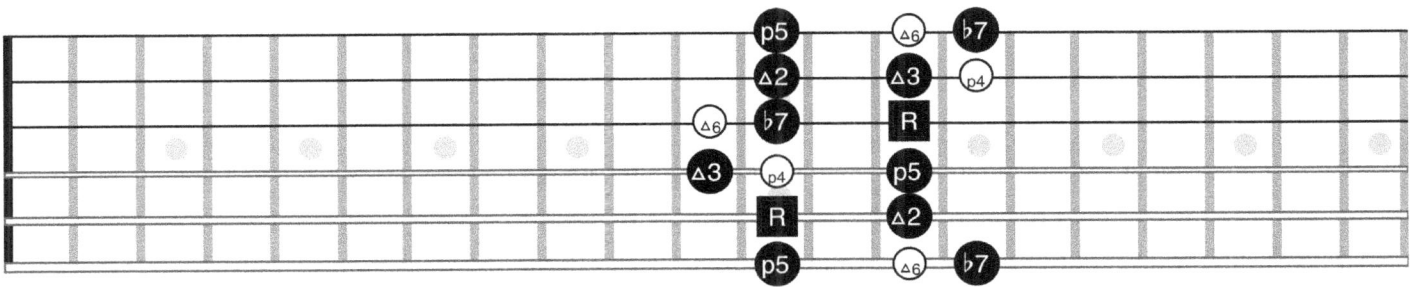

Shape 5

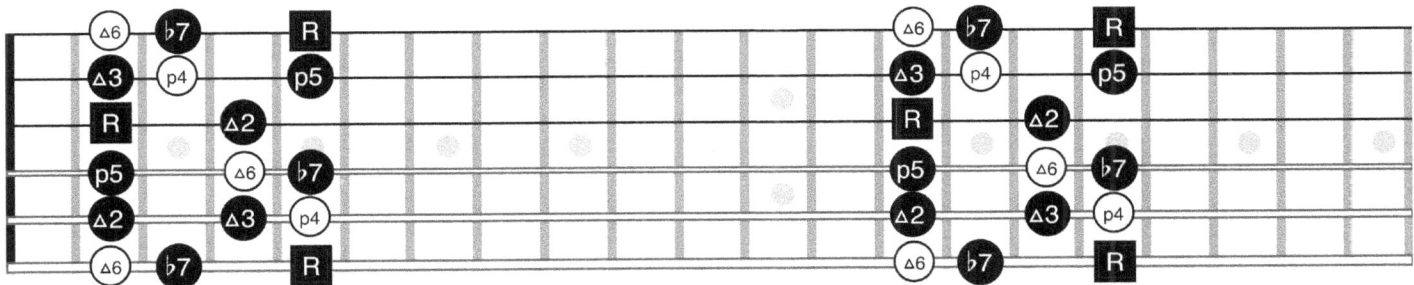

As with any scale, it's important to become secure in your *visual knowledge* of the Dominant Pentatonic. With that in mind, we'll begin with a series of exercises that will help you become sufficiently familiar with it before moving on to the various musical examples in subsequent chapters.

We'll then look at some effective exercises to help you visualise the Dominant Pentatonic in different keys within each area of the guitar neck. This will be a prelude to three solo studies. For each of these, you will be encouraged to consider the following aspects:

Vertical Motion, Lateral Motion and *Fast Sequences,* which we'll discuss as we progress.

Using these solos I will also introduce you to the following principles, which will help you to create musically balanced, interesting and exciting performances:

Narrative/Story. A solo should not sound like a collection of random, unrelated lines. Instead, it should be a chain of related musical statements that connect and develop in a smooth manner over the underlying chord progression.

Overall Shape. The first overall shape to master is one that builds. Structurally, it's no good coming in with all guns blazing, leaving yourself nowhere to go. Initially, it's best to start by easing into things gently and aim to build from there. Once you've developed the control to apply this structure, you can experiment with other variations.

Balance/Contrast. Every good solo or composition has elements of this. When learning the solo studies in this book, or constructing your own, think about developing a healthy balance of things like use of rhythms, space, dynamics and range, etc.

Expression & Articulation. Any solo will sound soulless and mechanical without these particular aspects. When listening to your favourite solos, take note of the ways in which life is breathed into the music via the use of bends, vibrato, slides, staccato notes, a mixture of picking and legato, harmonics, double-stops, etc.

Phrase-length & Starting Points. Some players are technically advanced but their phrasing is basic and repetitive (such as always playing two-bar phrases that start on the first beat of the bar, for example). When you study the solos in this book and listen to other solos, take note of both of these aspects to get a better understanding of how to produce a solo with a spontaneous, organic flow.

The Virtues of a Pre-written Solo. An improvised solo is an example of spontaneous composition, where some, or all, of the elements above are used to assemble an engaging, expressive musical statement on the spot. You can practice this slowly to increase your ability to do it spontaneously. After studying solos like the ones in this book, work at composing your own solos using the principles you've learned, and your ability to use these principles on the fly will grow over time. Developing vocabulary that you can associate with specific CAGED shapes will be a key factor in your progress.

Get the Audio

The audio files for this book are available to download for free from **www.fundamental-changes.com.** The link is in the top right-hand corner. Click on the "Guitar" link then simply select this book title from the drop-down menu and follow the instructions to get the audio.

We recommend that you download the files directly to your computer, not to your tablet, and extract them there before adding them to your media library.

For over 350 free guitar lessons with videos check out:

www.fundamental-changes.com

Join our free Facebook Community of Cool Musicians

www.facebook.com/groups/fundamentalguitar

Tag us for a share on Instagram: **FundamentalChanges**

Chapter One: Preparatory Exercises

This chapter teaches some useful exercises that will help you to effortlessly visualise the Dominant Pentatonic scale on the neck. They are not intended to be musically inspiring – their purpose is to give you a vital framework for learning the Dominant Pentatonic lines to come. View them as character-building homework before all the fun starts…like not being able to have dessert until you've finished your cabbage!

These sequences are written out in CAGED Shape 1, but you should apply them to all five shapes of A Dominant Pentatonic before eventually transposing everything to other keys.

You can rhythmically displace each exercise by playing any 1/16th note exercise as 1/8th note triplets and vice versa, though you may need to adjust the tempo accordingly.

Backing tracks are provided, but software tools such as *Transcribe!* are useful for looping them if you want to practice for longer.

To start with, here's an ascending three-note sequence played up and down through the scale.

Example 1a

You may notice that no fingerings are indicated for these patterns. It doesn't matter how you play them – the most important thing is that you train your eyes/brain to see where the notes are. Generally, I'm loathed to specify fingering choices for most things, as they will change depending on what you played before or where you are going next.

Next, here's the same approach, but with a descending three-note sequence from each scale note.

Example 1b

The following two exercises are the similar to the first two, but use four-note sequences launching from each note.

Example 1c

Example 1d

Fourths

An effective way of playing a pentatonic scale is to think about the *vertical forms* that exist within it. The diagram below shows all the notes of A Dominant Pentatonic stacked in a series of vertical arrangements.

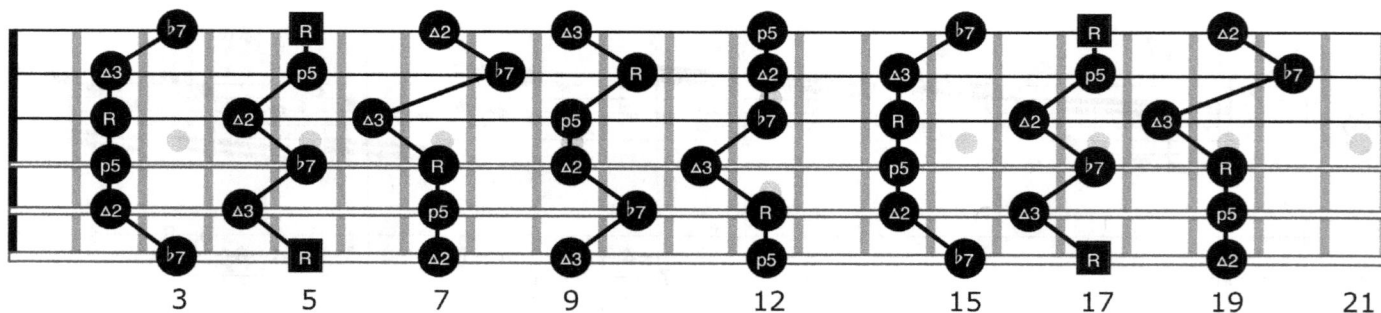

Although the consecutive stacked intervals within this scale vary between major 3rds, perfect 4ths and augmented 4ths, it's common for guitar players to refer to arranging pentatonic scales in this way as playing them in "fourths".

Playing "fourths" shapes within the Dominant Pentatonic poses both a visual and technical challenge, so it's useful to start with double-stops, as these require you to see two notes at the same time.

Example 1e

Barré Roll Technique

When played as single notes, pentatonic fourths often require you to play consecutive notes on adjacent strings within the same fret. When that happens, both notes can be played using a *barré roll* – playing two or more notes using the same finger. This is done by laying the finger across the relevant strings and redistributing its weight to press just one note at a time. Make sure that you roll your wrist and arm rather than distorting the finger, which should remain quite straight but slightly arched throughout.

Applying this technique to Example 1f is quite straightforward. In bar one, play the third note (7th fret) with the tip of the fourth finger, then play the fourth note on the adjacent string, 7th fret, with the pad of the fourth finger.

Example 1f

Using this technique on the next exercise requires a bit more forethought. Here, you will have to play the third note with the pad of the fourth finger, so there is enough finger left to play the fourth note using the tip. This is the approach you'll take whenever you use a *barré roll* to move from a higher pitched string to an adjacent lower pitched one.

Example 1g

Example 1h

Example 1i

Let's expand this idea to three-note stacks of fourths.

Example 1j shows Shape 1 of A Dominant Pentatonic played as three-note chords.

In certain styles, such as Fusion and Modern Jazz, these three-note clusters make effective chord options when *comping* (playing rhythm) over a static dominant chord and can be extended to larger note-groups to create four-note chords.

Example 1j

Let's use these three-note vertical clusters as the basis for a progressive series of single-note patterns.

Example 1k

Example 1l

Example 1m

Example 1n

For the purposes of this book, we will stop at three-note stacks, but feel free to explore four-, five-, and six-note stacks too.

Chapter Two: Vertical Motion

On guitar, *vertical motion* is the practice of playing within one area of the neck, i.e., moving from string to string within the same fret area, rather than shifting along the length of the neck.

A7 CAGED Lines Featuring Vertical Motion

This first line is based around CAGED Shape 1 of A Dominant Pentatonic. Here, we're giving some expression to this straight 1/16th note passage by adding a bend, a slide, and some vibrato.

Example 2a

Next, from the fourth note of bar one, the melody spells out a series of descending fourths – in this case, down one and then up the next (as practiced in the second half of Example 1g).

Again, we're in Shape 1, but this time we're adding interest by using broken and *syncopated* (offbeat) rhythms.

Notice how the line extends into Shape 2 with the C# note on the first string at the 21st fret.

Example 2b

Like the previous example, the following CAGED Shape 2 line features broken rhythms and fourths (in the first half of bar two).

Adding vibrato to various notes is not only a way to add expression, it's an effective means of practicing solid finger placement. Play up and down a scale adding vibrato to every note. If your finger placement isn't good, your finger will slip off when you try to add vibrato. This is also a great way of working and strengthening your fretting hand.

Example 2c

Moving up to CAGED Shape 3, this line moves down through the scale using an ascending four-note sequence from each new starting note. It applies the same principle demonstrated in the second half of Example 1c.

Example 2d

Example 2e shows a straightforward use of the approach used in examples 2b and 2c, as we travel down one fourth and up the next. This time, we're just playing straight 1/16th notes with no rests.

Every time you have to play consecutive notes at the 12th fret, use a *barré roll* by fretting the first note with the fingerprint part of the third finger, so there is enough finger left over to play the second note using the tip of the same finger.

Example 2e

This example ascends the full length of Shape 3. The constant stream of 1/16th notes is given expression using a combination of approaches (ascending four-note sequence, accented notes, pull-offs, vibrato etc) which stop it from sounding predictable.

The first bar begins with an ascending four-note sequence from each note (first demonstrated in Example 1c).

Example 2f

This Shape 4 example starts with the simple melodic device of hitting certain notes more than once in succession (a favourite approach of fusion guitarist Scott Henderson).

Bar one of this example is also based on fourth shapes with adjacent note-pairs throughout, so use *barré roll* movements here too.

The whole thing ends with an ascending run in Shape 4 arranged in a 2-1-2-1-2-1 note-configuration (a favourite approach of players like Jazz-Fusion guitarist Tim Miller), followed by a descending equivalent in Shape 5.

Example 2g

The first two bars of this next Shape 4 example demonstrate the opposite approach to that used in Example 2d. Here, we're ascending the scale, but playing a descending-four-note sequence from each new starting note (as in the first half of Example 1d).

In bars 3-4, the descending four-note sequence is continued from each new starting note (from G onwards), but this time while descending the scale (as in the second half of Example 1d).

The line concludes in bar five with the A Minor Pentatonic scale (A, C, D, E, G) to finish off in a bluesy manner.

Example 2h

Still in Shape 4, this line uses double-stops in bar one, combined with ear-catching hammer-ons. The line then takes a short detour to Shape 3 before ending back in Shape 4, where a mixture of pull-offs, slides, accented notes, and vibrato is used to add expression and interest.

Example 2i

More double-stops are used in this Shape 4 line which features a syncopated rhythm most players would probably play using hybrid picking (as shown in the notation, though I used a pick throughout on the recorded example). This example finishes up in Shape 5.

Example 2j

The last of our Shape 4 lines demonstrates a simple but effective use of string skips. In other words, it's quite easy to play, but sounds great!

Example 2k

Moving up to Shape 5, this line begins with an approach mirroring that of the Shape 3 melody in Example 2f (a four-note ascending sequence followed by some accented notes). It ends by ascending the same 2-1-2-1-2-1 note-configuration used in the final bar of Example 2g.

Example 2l

Finally, Example 2m features a mixture of the various approaches used so far, including wide interval skips in the first two beats of bar one based around an E minor arpeggio (E, G, B). It starts in Shape 5 and finishes in Shape 1.

If you experience difficulty playing the five-note groupings at the end of bar two, revisit this example after studying Chapter Three.

Example 2m

Chapter Three: Note-Groupings

Before we move on to exploring *lateral motion* using the Dominant Pentatonic Scale, I want you to study a technique that is useful for producing melodic variety in longer lines.

When playing constant 1/16th notes, by repeating musical motifs ("note groupings") that are not divisible by 4, we can create a constant shift of emphasis known as *rhythmic displacement*.

For example, look what happens when a five-note grouping is repeated using four even notes per beat.

Notice how the accented first note of each group moves position throughout the groupings.

If we count a bar of 1/16th notes as "**1**-e-&-a, **2**-e-&-a, **3**-e-&-a, **4**-e-&-a", the first note of the first group falls on beat 1 of bar one. The first note of the second group falls on the "e" of beat 2. The first note of the third group falls on the "& of beat 3, and the first note of the fourth group falls on the very last note of bar one (the "a" of beat 4) so that this five-note grouping crosses the bar line.

It takes a full five bars before note 1 of a five-note group falls on beat 1 of a bar.

The advantages of using a rhythmic approach like this are twofold:

- **It reduces the amount of thought required.** Instead of having to be endlessly creative while playing a long line, *rhythmic displacement* does all the work for you as the emphasis shifts automatically. Paradoxically, it's a technique that allows us to repeat a figure without it sounding repetitive, thus maintaining the listener's interest.

- **It gives each line an inner musical logic.** This helps to make it sound cohesive and "right". In other words, the notes sound like they belong together even though the listener can't work out why.

Although this technique has many musical advantages, it can be technically challenging as it requires a form of rhythmic "spatial awareness". The acid test is that you must be able to tap your foot on each quarter-note throughout the phrase as the accents of the repeating phrase shift underneath you. If you can tap your foot accurately on the beat, it means that you remain well-grounded rhythmically – like an acrobat who instinctively knows where the floor is mid-somersault.

If you experience difficulty, break down each example beat by beat, establish the contents of each quarter-note, and then practice inching your way from one beat to the next.

Rhythmic displacement will occur whenever your melodic note-groupings are not divisible by the rhythmic subdivision you are playing. For example, groupings of 2, 4, 5 and 7 notes will create interesting displacements when playing 1/8th note triplets (three notes per beat).

A7 CAGED Lines Featuring Note-Groupings

Let's begin with a line that features a series of three-note groupings in Shape 3 of A Dominant Pentatonic.

It is a scale sequence that we first encountered in Example 1b but we're no longer playing triplets. Instead, we're playing 1/16th notes divided into three-note groups.

Start by isolating and repeating the four notes in each beat before trying to string them together. When you do so, your foot should be tapping accurately on each beat, rather than on the start of each three-note group. Use a metronome to help you focus on where your foot should land.

Example 3a

This line also features three-note groupings played in straight 1/16th notes. Now, the scale is arranged three notes per string and spans an area straddling Shapes 4 and 5. Note the descending string skips in the second half of the line.

Example 3b

Four-note groupings fit perfectly into our 1/16th note count, and therefore don't create any rhythmic displacement, so let's jump straight into playing five-note groupings.

Example 3c is based around a repeated lick in Shape 1.

The grace note at the start of each grouping has no rhythmic value, which leaves us with notes totalling five 1/16th notes per grouping. As we discussed earlier, five-note motifs take a long time (five bars) to cycle back to their starting point.

To learn this line, start by targeting the note that corresponds to your foot falling on the second beat of bar one (the final note of the first five-note lick). Then play until the note that corresponds to your foot falling on the third beat of that bar (the penultimate note in the second five-note lick), etc.

Continue this process, then start stringing beats together, making sure that you hit all the relevant checkpoints with both your fingers and foot. Slow things right down and practice to a metronome at first, then gradually increase the tempo to that of the backing track.

Example 3c

This line switches between Shape 1 and Shape 5 of the scale. Each five-note motif is constructed using the same 2-1-2 note-configuration across three strings. Again, if you experience difficulty playing the line while tapping your foot on the beat, start by practicing slowly from beat to beat before gradually stringing everything together.

You might find it easier to use a hammer-on on each two-note grouping.

Example 3d

Note the use of string skips in bar two of the following Shape 4 line, which is adapted from the pentatonic riff in one of my tunes, *Act of Faith*.

Example 3e

The next Shape 5 example takes the repeated motif from Example 3c (an 1/8th note followed by three 1/16th notes) down through a vertical scale shape.

This is a modified version of the scale sequence first demonstrated in the second half of Example 1d.

Example 3f

In Example 3g, each motif totals six 1/16th notes (comprised of five 1/16th notes and two 1/32nd notes). In bar two, the line deviates from Dominant Pentatonic into a bluesy A Dorian phrase.

Notice the chromatic passing note (F natural) used as a bridge between the E and F# notes.

(N.B. In the notation, a * symbol will be placed above any chromatic note from here onwards).

In this book, chromatic notes will always function in one of the following ways:

- a chromatic approach-note from either a semi-tone or above or below a target note.

- a means of chromatically bridging between one scale note and another.

You can learn much more about applying chromatic notes in my book *Chromatic Lead Guitar Techniques*.

Example 3g

Next, we move on to seven-note groupings (in this case, each comprising six 1/16th note and two 1/32nd notes, which adds up to seven 1/16th notes).

This line shifts from Shape 1 down through Shape 5 to Shape 4.

Each CAGED shape is extended on the first string, as playing three notes per string always involves borrowing from the shape above. For example, although centred around Shape 1, the first seven-note motif also uses notes in Shape 2.

The penultimate note in bar two is a C (a b3 interval over the chord), which is tweaked towards the more consonant C# via a "curl" (a quarter-tone bend) to create a bluesy effect. These final two notes are drawn from the A Minor Pentatonic scale.

Example 3h

Since eight-note groupings are divisible by four they don't displace when repeated, so we'll jump straight to nine-note groupings.

The six-note pick-up line to this next example is an ascending A7 arpeggio (A, C#, E, G) with a chromatic C approach note to the C#.

In bar one, the first grouping contains all five pitches of A Dominant Pentatonic on the top two strings. This grouping is shifted down an octave using the same fingering on the middle two strings, then down another octave to the bottom string-pair.

This three-octave symmetrical motion is convenient on guitar, and a principle exploited by every piano player over many more octaves than just three.

Example 3i

This example uses ten-note groupings and the same three-octave symmetrical fingering principle, but this time we ascend from the base of Shape 3 up through Shapes 4 and 5 to Shape 1.

Example 3j

This ten-note grouping is in the form of a repeated three-notes-per-string lick that straddles Shapes 4 and 5. Generally, I always associate this kind of idea as belonging to the lower shape (in this case Shape 4) but extending into the one above (Shape 5).

Example 3k

Next, we move on to eleven-note groupings. The first idea uses the three-octave symmetrical approach across the top, middle and bottom string-pairs.

This example starts in the top of Shape 5 and shifts down through Shape 4 to finish in a pretty straightforward ascent of Shape 3.

Example 3l

In this eleven-note grouping we apply this principle to a three-notes-per-string pattern that spans Shapes 4 and 5 and uses string skipping.

Example 3m

We finish with a line that uses twelve-note groupings and three-octave symmetrical fingering. Note how I finish with a bluesy A Minor Pentatonic scale for the last two notes.

Example 3n

Chapter Four: Lateral Motion

In this chapter, we are going to look at lines that move along the length of the guitar neck (*lateral motion*).

To practice lateral motion, we will play a short phrase in one position, then shift to a new position to play a similar idea using notes from the same scale. This will force us to adjust the intervals of the original idea to stay within the scale.

Lateral motion has several advantages:

- The same picking and fingering configuration can be maintained throughout.

- It helps you to generate more musical material.

- It encourages thematic development in your playing.

- Your tone stays uniform as the same string-groups are used throughout.

- Lateral motion is often more expressive than vertical motion because it is possible to add more nuance over the same musical distance.

To understand that last point, consider the octave interval between two A notes in the following positions:

- The A at the 17th fret of the first string, and the A on the 14th fret of the third string.

- The A at the 17th fret of the first string, and the A on the 5th fret of the same string.

The notes are both an octave apart, but when travelling along the length of the top string there is an array of nuances (bends, trills, slides, etc) that can be used to embellish a melody. When played across multiple strings the same distance can seem to pass by in a flash.

A7 CAGED Lines Featuring Lateral Motion

Let's look at two lines that feature motifs played on adjacent strings.

This first one stems from Shape 1 and shifts up the guitar neck to an equivalent shape an octave higher, using adjacent "fourth" shapes. Each motif comprises three notes and, when played in straight 1/16th notes, creates a "three-over-four" rhythmic effect. This particular form of rhythmic displacement is known as a *hemiola*.

As you climb the neck, place everything that you play in context by visualising how the notes relate to each of the underlying CAGED positions.

Example 4a

The next example descends from Shape 2 to settle in Shape 4.

In bar one, we link parallel pentatonic fourth shapes again on the top two strings. However, the first note of each beat is a chromatic approach from a semi-tone below (shown with an *). Towards the end of bar one, we then transition into another descending fourth-based sequence.

Example 4b

The next two examples feature motifs that span three strings.

We start by stacking three adjacent pentatonic fourths in Shape 1, before shifting them up the neck through each CAGED shape. This is a lateral interpretation of the idea used in Example 1k, but the rhythm here is an 1/8th note followed by two 1/6th notes.

The line finishes with a simple descent of Shape 1.

Example 4c

Example 4d uses a series of five-note groupings that produce a durable form of rhythmic displacement to help maintain interest.

Here, the scale is arranged in three-notes-per-string form and played in a 2-1-2 note-configuration, formed by skipping every other note. If you're not used to this sort of approach, you might find the stretches quite challenging. Practice playing anything involving wide stretches in short bursts to prevent straining your hand.

Example 4d

Now we have the first of six examples that span three strings and contain string skips.

This one begins in Shape 2 and uses a series of double-stops that are either a major sixth or a minor seventh, depending on where you are in the scale. As you shift along the neck, remember to place everything you play in context by visualising how the notes relate to each CAGED shape.

Example 4e

The following example starts in Shape 3 and concludes with a straightforward descent of Shape 1. The syncopated rhythm created by the accented notes on the top string is also used in Examples 4h and 4m.

Example 4f

This idea also features string skips and rhythmic displacement. I play a hammer-on at the start, but you can ignore that if you like, as the main figure is picked. Pay attention to the quick, first-finger position shifts linking each six-note grouping.

Example 4g

Next, we have a series of accented eight-note groupings that use string-skips.

View the three-notes-per-string shapes as occupying two CAGED shapes at the same time. It begins by straddling Shapes 5 and 1, then Shapes 5 and 4, and finishes with a two-notes-per-string idea in Shape 3.

Example 4h

The previous four examples used string-skips on the top three strings but now we're going to skip the third string instead.

Each six-note motif is derived from a three-notes-per-string approach and produces rhythmic displacement. We start off straddling Shapes 2 and 3 and finish in Shape 3.

If we represent the six pitches within each grouping played in ascending order (from lowest to highest) as 123456, then the note-order in each of the three six-note motifs in this example is 162453 (just one of 720 possible mathematical permutations when playing six different pitches once each. Have fun exploring these!)

Example 4i

In this example, each nine-note grouping is created by omitting the middle pitch of a three-notes-per-string pattern. The accents in each nine-note grouping are a development of the ones used in the eight-note groupings in Examples 4f, 4h and 4m.

Example 4j

Here's another example featuring nine-note motifs. Each one spans four strings and is created by stacking intervals from a three-notes-per-string approach. It begins by straddling Shapes 4 and 5 and finishes in Shape 2. It ends in bar three with a blues curl (quarter-tone bend) on the C note (b3).

I played this line with a combination of sweep picking, *barré rolls* and legato.

Example 4k

This is the first of two examples featuring ideas that span five strings using string-skips, and draws upon three-notes-per-string shapes.

The notes of the initial sixteen-note motif are adapted to fit the scale as it is shifted up the neck to a new position. It begins by straddling Shapes 4 and 5 in bar one and moves to Shapes 5 and 1 in bar two.

Example 4l

This final line begins by straddling Shapes 3 and 4 in the first half of bar one, then moves up to an equivalent eight-note sequence straddling Shapes 4 and 5 in the second half.

As with Example 4j, we omit the middle of the three notes on each string to create some wide melodic stretches. Once again, we conclude with a bit of bluesy earthiness.

Example 4m

Chapter Five: Fast Sequences

So far, all our lines have been medium paced, but in the interest of balance it's important to develop some fast ideas too.

Playing fast sequences often requires a variety of approaches, such as two-, three- and four-notes-per-string arrangements of notes, legato, right-hand tapping, left-hand-tapping, etc. When learning to master these techniques in a specific scale shape, it's important to work on finding various entry and exit points to the sequence, so that you can flow from one idea into another confidently. Also, when working on vocabulary for a particular CAGED shape, you should start by looking at how you can combine it with your existing Mixolydian and Blues scale vocabulary in the same area.

Legato techniques feature more prominently as the tempo increases, so in the notation of the following examples you will notice the appearance of the following:

- **Circle around a note** – meaning it should be played using a right-hand tap.

- **Square around a note** – played using a left-hand tap (also known as a "hammer-on from nowhere").

A7 CAGED Lines Featuring Fast Sequences

Example 5a is the first of three two-notes-per-string examples using the A Dominant Pentatonic scale.

In bar two, I use a succession of descending six-note patterns in Shape 4, similar to those used by players like Shawn Lane. You can try creating a line using an equivalent ascending idea.

The final note (E) is reached via a whole step bend from below (the note D, from A Minor Pentatonic).

Example 5a

Next is the repetition of a twelve-note 1/16th note triplet sequence in Shape 5 that transitions up to Shape 1 at the end. It is an adapted version of one that Uli Jon Roth (Scorpions) originally played using the Phrygian Dominant scale in the intro to *Sails of Charon*.

Example 5b

The final two-notes-per-string idea is based around Shape 4 and uses *barré rolls* to play two consecutive notes on adjacent strings – an approach often used by Greg Howe and Ritchie Kotzen. Don't be too concerned about keeping the notes separate. If they ring together the intervals create a characteristic Rock 'n' Roll grind that's different to (for example) playing the same thing with tapping.

Example 5c

The next approaches span two CAGED shapes at the same time. The first uses wide stretches and straddles Shapes 4 and 5, then finishes in Shape 5.

Each descending quintuplet motif is created by playing every other note of a three-notes-per-string shape, resulting in a 2-1-2 note-configuration on each three-string group.

Bar one is a descending equivalent of the start of Example 3d, whereas bar two is a rhythmically displaced version of the second half of Example 1b (played as 1/16th notes instead of 1/8th note triples).

Example 5d

This example uses a three-notes-per-string approach (again, straddling Shapes 4 and 5), but has a simple but effective three-note Van Halen-style tapping motif on each string. Here, the notes are batched in groups of nine, leading to a less repetitive-sounding pattern.

The final bend (on a right-hand tap) extends into Shape 1 and should be supported on the same string by a bend at the 15th fret by the fretting hand.

Think of the right-hand taps as beating out a repeated three-note 1/8th note rhythm spread over two bars.

Example 5e

I was tempted to leave this example until the end, because the four-notes-per-string shape is somewhat challenging, but in reality it isn't much more difficult than the three-notes-per-string examples that follow.

Playing four-notes-per-string (and straddling three pentatonic shapes at the same time) requires a panoramic vision of the neck and visualising three CAGED shapes at the same time. It's a great way of unlocking the fingerboard.

In beat 3 of bar two a G# (shown with an asterisk) is used as a chromatic bridge between the A and G notes.

Example 5f

Played using three-notes-per-string (straddling Shapes 4 and 5), this example features an intricate interplay between left- and right-hand tapping typical of Greg Howe. As in Example 5e, right-hand taps beat out a constant 1/8th note rhythm.

Example 5g

This Greg Howe-style ascending sequence is the ascending equivalent of the previous example.

The right-hand taps a constant 1/8th note rhythm, so it's the left-hand taps that are the problem as they occur on the first finger and so require a high and purposeful placement to create enough strength/volume.

Practice learning and repeating just three notes at a time before stringing everything together.

Example 5h

Let's introduce some string-skips. The passage in the first bar of the next example straddles Shapes 3 and 4 and is shifted laterally up the neck in the following bar to straddle Shapes 4 and 5, where an equivalent sequence is played. The line shifts to Shape 5 in bars 3-4, and takes a more traditional two-notes-per-string approach.

This particular example is the first of several that require you to play the first note on a new string with a left-hand tap using the first finger. Playing strong taps without incurring any extraneous noise often means retraining the fingers out of certain rogue tendencies.

Combining right-hand taps and left-hand "hammer-ons-from-nowhere" provides a distinct advantage when ascending a scale, as your fretting hand can leave the fretboard each time a right-hand tap is played, allowing the first finger to strike the note from a sufficient height to create a strong note when starting a new string.

To do this successfully, you must follow a particular sequence of movements. Let's use the start of bar one as an example:

- Play the initial 10th and 12th frets using hammer-ons with the left hand (first and second, or first and third fingers. The third may be easier to begin with).

- When you tap the B note at the 14th fret with the right hand, the left hand should simultaneously spring up so that it is poised to come down on the 9th fret of the third string from height.

- When your first finger taps the 9th fret of the third string, it's important that your right hand doesn't spring up simultaneously from the 14th fret of the fifth string, as this will create unwanted open-string noise. Instead, as the left-hand taps, *soften* your contact with the right-hand tapped note on the string without actually leaving it. This will stop it from vibrating and allow you to gently remove your finger without any unwanted noise. It can also help if you damp the string with the side of the picking hand (karate-chop-style).

This sequence is continued throughout the scale every time you move to a thinner string with a left-hand tap. Practice the sequence slowly as you'll need to program this precise set of movements before speeding up.

Example 5i

Example 5j takes a similar approach but is confined to the fifth and third strings. It features the same sort of lateral movement, and the two-beat, thirteen-note motif is modified to stay within the scale as I shift up the neck.

As always, make sure that you relate everything you play to the underlying CAGED shape(s). You might feel this slows you down at first, but you will reap the benefits in the long run as your ability to contextualise what you play speeds up.

Example 5j

There are more of the same elements here but this time we're on the third and first strings. We start in Shape 3 and ascend laterally through Shapes 4, 5 and 1, ending with a blues-style Minor Pentatonic phrase.

Example 5k

Example 51 is the descending equivalent of the previous example and starts with the fretting hand in Shape 5.

In bar two, the right-hand tap bend (16th fret) is supported with a bend on the 12th fret of the same string with the fretting hand. The vibrato on that bend also comes from the fretting-hand bend at the 12th fret.

Example 51

We finish with another four-notes-per-string idea that spans CAGED Shapes 4, 5 and 1.

Rhythmically, it's septuplets (seven notes per beat) throughout. Target the note at the start of each beat and space the notes between as evenly as possible. The internal rhythms should take care of themselves.

Example 5m

Chapter Six: Running the Changes

The progression used for the first two solo studies in chapters seven and eight is a series of dominant 7 chords. Our melodic ideas will therefore be drawn from the corresponding Mixolydian scale for each chord, and the Dominant Pentatonic framework that exists inside it.

A Mixolydian		C Mixolydian		D Mixolydian		F Mixolydian		G Mixolydian	
A7 / / /	/ / / /	C7 / / /	/ / / /	D7 / / /	/ / / /	F7 / / /	/ / / /	G7 / / /	/ / / /

Here are the notes of those five Mixolydian scales and the Dominant Pentatonic scales within each one.

A Mixolydian	A	B	C#	D	E	F#	G
A Dominant Pentatonic	A	B	C#		E		G
Formula	1	2	3	4	5	6	b7

C Mixolydian	C	D	E	F	G	A	Bb
C Dominant Pentatonic	C	D	E		G		Bb
Formula	1	2	3	4	5	6	b7

D Mixolydian	D	E	F#	G	A	B	C
D Dominant Pentatonic	D	E	F#		A		C
Formula	1	2	3	4	5	6	b7

F Mixolydian	F	G	A	Bb	C	D	Eb
F Dominant Pentatonic	F	G	A		C		Eb
Formula	1	2	3	4	5	6	b7

G Mixolydian	G	A	B	C	D	E	F
G Dominant Pentatonic	G	A	B		D		F
Formula	1	2	3	4	5	6	b7

Transposing Dominant Pentatonic CAGED Shapes

To prepare for the solos you should practice transposing each of the A Mixolydian and A Dominant Pentatonic CAGED shapes to the other five keys of the solo.

Focus on the root note of each shape and shift it *up* or *down* to relocate the whole pattern to the appropriate area of the fretboard.

- For **C7**, shift any A Dominant Pentatonic/Mixolydian shape up 3 frets or down 9 frets.

- For **D7**, shift any A Dominant Pentatonic/Mixolydian shape up 5 frets or down 7 frets.

- For **F7**, shift any A Dominant Pentatonic/Mixolydian shape up 8 frets or down 4 frets.

- For **G7**, shift any A Dominant Pentatonic/Mixolydian shape up 10 frets or down 2 frets.

Playing in One Area

The next step is to practice changing scales while staying in one area of the neck by finding the appropriate CAGED shape for each chord/scale.

The following table shows which CAGED shapes for A7, C7, D7, F7 and G7 exist in each neck position (roughly defined by the dot markers on the fretboard).

Fret Area (dot markers)	A7	C7	D7	F7	G7
5th – 7th Fret or (17th-19th)	Shape 1	Shape 5	Shape 4	Shape 3	Shape 2
7th – 9th Fret	Shape 2	Shape 1	Shape 5	Shape 4	Shape 3
9th – 12th Fret	Shape 3	Shape 2	Shape 1	Shape 5	Shape 4
12th – 15th Fret	Shape 4	Shape 3	Shape 2	Shape 1	Shape 5
15th – 17th Fret or (3rd – 5th)	Shape 5	Shape 4	Shape 3	Shape 2	Shape 1

The following exercises demonstrate a way to run through Dominant Pentatonic scales in all five keys around the 5th-7th fret area. When you feel confident playing in this region, apply the exercises to each area shown in the table.

As you are getting to grips with this, feel free to learn these changes slowly in free time, as it's a lot of work. But you should soon move on to playing them with a metronome and without stopping between each chord, since playing over key changes involves being able to visualise both the scale you are playing and the scale you are going to play next, at the same time. Working with a metronome will ensure you don't allow yourself any thinking time between one chord and the next.

In terms of fingering, I advise that you place your first finger on the lowest note of each string.

Backing tracks are provided so that you can hear each scale in context.

Example 6a:

A7 (A Dominant Pentatonic shape 1)   C7 (C Dominant Pentatonic shape 5)

D7 (D Dominant Pentatonic shape 4)   F7 (F Dominant Pentatonic shape 3)

G7 (G Dominant Pentatonic shape 2)

Example 6b:

As there are five different chords in this sequence, the final exercise takes two cycles to complete. You'll start by ascending the A7 chord in the first half (bar one) but descend it in the second half (bar six).

Example 6c:

F7 (F Dominant Pentatonic shape 3)   **G7** (G Dominant Pentatonic shape 2)

Linking chords

The previous exercises were designed to develop your ability to visualise each scale shape. They did not, however, teach you to make elegant *musical* transitions from one scale to the next while playing lines, sequences or licks. The aim of the following solos is therefore to teach you to play smoothly *through* the key changes, rather than playing statically up and down each one.

As you listen to each solo study, ask yourself, would a non-musician know that the underlying progression was in five different keys?

My musical phrases and ideas often begin over one chord and conclude over the next. This involves adapting to the new scale "mid phrase", so that the direction/intention of the original line is left relatively undisturbed. It's a bit like being a waiter with a tray of drinks trying to get to a distant table – just because you encounter an obstacle you shouldn't end up in the street! Instead, you need to manoeuvre around elegantly while maintaining a clear sense of your original destination (and not spilling drinks on your customers!)

Keep this in mind as you work your way through each transcription and focus on how I transition melodically between the five different scales.

Chapter Seven: Vertical Motion Solo Study

Using Prepared Lines when Improvising

As a soloist your aim should be to build an arsenal of shapes, licks and lines in each CAGED shape, so that you have some flexible friends to draw upon when improvising.

This can only be achieved by going beyond playing each line verbatim. A line simply represents a useful contour/chain of events, and you need to learn to interpret it in a multitude of different ways, depending on the musical setting.

For this reason, it is good to practice limiting your playing to just one line and see how much variation you can get from it, so that it works at any given moment.

Take a single line you like from the previous chapters and try the following:

- Start it differently.

- Break off half-way through.

- Change the ending.

- Change the timing/rhythm.

- Try playing it backwards.

When improvising, it's better to have ten lines that you can adapt in a variety of ways than to be at the mercy of 500 "licks" that are set in stone. The latter limits your approach to mentally scrolling through a massive list of licks, frantically hoping to pull one off the shelf that will provide you with the perfect musical moment. It's hardly the grounds for fluid spontaneity! However, the first approach will always create musically appropriate moments, even though the ideas stem from the same creative concept.

Creating a Solo

When I recorded the following two solos, I had a loose set of ideas (lines, sequences and licks) I intended to use, which outlined the Dominant Pentatonic material I wanted to highlight. That was my starting point. From there, I played over each backing track and tried to produce a series of related musical events which had a natural flow and didn't sound contrived.

When composing these sorts of solo studies, I often try various approaches, then just immerse myself in the moment and record what comes out.

I then listen back to the recordings, pick out the best bits, and shuffle them into what my creative brain says is some sort of logical, musical order. Once they are laid out, I then compose and record transitional material that links each section together.

If some strong themes have emerged in this process, I will go back into the backing track and start "framing" those ideas by crafting specific drum and bass fills and/or adding harmony parts (e.g., via the keyboards) to make them bolder and lock in with the track. *Voila!*

Doing it this way means that I get to respond to the precise sound of the guitar and the tempo, feel and nature of the music

Vertical Motion Solo Study Analysis

Because the following solo is annotated, much of it will be self-explanatory, so this bar-by-bar analysis refers to other points of interest.

When soloing, it's normal to combine the Dominant Pentatonic with other scales, like the Major/Minor Pentatonic and Mixolydian, rather than use it in isolation. Consequently, these ideas have been set alongside Mixolydian to create a well-balanced, natural musical setting.

Modulation

When a backing track is in five different keys, it's important to develop a variety of techniques for negotiating the transitions between them to create melodies that have a continuous, convincing flow, and are unhampered by the changes.

The following table outlines the various options available. I will highlight these in the analysis if/when they occur within the solo.

TRANSITION (MODULATION) BETWEEN KEYS
1) **Semi-tone resolution:** from the old scale to the new one.
2) **Delayed first phrase in new key:** leave a gap at the start of the new key change.
3) **Common notes:** join two keys with note(s) that are common to both.
4) **Anticipation:** play a note of the new key early and hold it over the bar line.
5) **Short "pick-up" played in new key over the last part of the preceding chord/key:** for example, start a C7 phrase in the last bar of the preceding A7 section using notes that relate to C7. Any tension produced at the end of the A7 chord will be resolved with the arrival of the C7.
6) **Short "pick-up" played at the end of the previous chord in that key, which then leads to the new key:** for example, start a C7 phrase in the last bar of the preceding A7 section using notes that relate to A7.
7) **Long phrase across two or more keys that modulates halfway through:** your line should modulate seamlessly during the key change, keeping its sense of direction both melodically and rhythmically. This is an extended version of the shorter "pick-up" principle mentioned above.
8) **An idea that metamorphosizes through the changes:** repeat a motif and adapt it to fit any new key(s).

Bars 1-2

As I improvised this solo study some of my playing quirks revealed themselves when I transcribed what I played. One of these is my habit of using a particular form of chromatic embellishment.

I begin with just such a move where there is a fleeting slide down from a chromatic Bb note (indicated with an asterisk). This is just an expressive way of introducing the following A note. The same movement also crops up again in bars eighteen, twenty-eight and thirty.

I use modulation Option 6 here, as the five-note pick-up relating to A7 forms part of the long phrase in bars 3-4.

Bars 3-4

These bars contain Example 2f transposed from A to C.

Both solo studies feature some *semi-harmonics* (S.H). Unlike *pinched harmonics*, a semi-harmonic retains the main note/pitch but adds some harmonic "glitter" around it. I create this effect by dragging the face of my second fingernail across the string as I pick it with the plectrum. It's a great way to add vocal expression by "opening the mouth" of the sound, and creates an effect similar to Brian May's tone.

Bars 5-6

Some bars do not feature any Dominant Pentatonic scales (namely bars five, six, and 25-26). These add some balance between the different elements, and I simply chose to use the full Mixolydian scale here because it felt right at the time.

Bar five demonstrates Option 2 from our modulation table above, whereby I allow the new key to establish itself before starting to play.

Bars 13-14

There is an extreme example of anticipation here as three notes of D Dominant Pentatonic are played at the end of bar 14 in anticipation of the D7 in the following bar (Option 5). An asterisk shows the Eb chromatic note in bar 14.

Bars 15-16

This section features Example 2k transposed to D and starting from the end of bar 14.

I used my whammy bar for the vibrato on the second double-stop in bar 16, but you can just apply it using your fretting hand if your guitar isn't fitted with a bar.

Bars 19-20

Bar twenty contains a long line derived from the first two octaves of a three-octave symmetrical shape that continues into the following bar with three notes from the new key (Option 7).

Bars 21-22

Bar twenty-two features the second bar of Example 2m. The line resolves by a semi-tone to C Dominant Pentatonic at the start of the following section (Option 1).

Bars 23-24

The open D string at the end of bar twenty-four is played in anticipation of the subsequent D7 chord.

Bars 27-28

The second half of bar twenty-eight is like the second half of Example 1d.

This section uses modulation Options 3 and 4 at the end of the bar, where a D note is tied over the bar. D is the fifth of G7, but is also common to the preceding F Dominant Pentatonic.

Bars 29-30

This passage uses a pedal point in bar twenty-nine (with a moving line under the static G) and a vertical representation of the scale in bar thirty, mainly comprising stacked fifth and fourth intervals.

The final note in bar thirty is played using both a semi-harmonic and *glissando* vibrato. The latter involves sliding back and forth over the note (in this case A) by about a semitone either side. Note the "tail-off" where I conclude by sliding a short way up the length of the string.

Bars 31-40

This final chorus adds a flute-like harmony and demonstrates how it is possible to take an initial idea (bars 31-32) and adapt the notes to fit each new chord while staying in the same area of the neck (Option 8 from our modulation table).

I use a different CAGED shape for each chord: A7 (Shape 5), C7 (Shape 4), D7 (Shape 3), F7 (Shape 2) and G7 (Shape 1), consistent with the final row of the CAGED grid in Chapter Six.

Remember to relate *everything* you play to the underlying CAGED shape, or the notes will be meaningless, and stop you transferring these ideas to other keys.

Balance

It is important to present a balanced range of contrasting elements to sustain the listener's interest and make any solo engaging from start to finish.

With this in mind, the table below provides another layer of analysis that shows how I introduce these features as part of the composition process:

MUSICAL ELEMENTS	BARS (examples)
Attack: legato vs picking.	six
Articulation: plain notes vs ones with vibrato, bends, slides etc.	Twenty-two vs twenty-three
Dynamics: notes of even volume vs accented ones.	Two vs three
Rhythms: straight subdivisions vs syncopated ones.	Fifteen vs twenty-nine
Note Placement: straight notes vs tied and/or dotted notes.	First half of four vs second half of four
Range: low notes vs high ones.	One vs end of four
Melodic contrast: close intervals vs wide intervals.	First half of thirty vs second half of thirty
Phrase-length: short vs long.	One vs 3-4
Texture: single-notes vs double-stops.	Fifteen vs sixteen
Note duration: long notes vs staccato ones.	Nine vs twenty-nine
Note density: space (low density) vs lots of notes (high density).	Twenty-one vs twenty-two

Vertical Motion Solo Study

(S.H. = semi-harmonic)   P.H. = pinched harmonic)

Shaun Baxter

A Dominant Pentatonic with Bb passing note

A Dom. Pent.

C Dominant Pentatonic

S.H.

Loco

D Mixolydian

F Dominant Pentatonic

S.H.

G Dominant Pentatonic

A Dominant Pentatonic

A Mixolydian

BU

C Dominant Pentatonic with Eb passing note

ARP

S.H.

D Dominant Pentatonic

w.bar

Loco

Loco

F Dominant Pentatonic with Ab passing note

G Dominant Pentatonic

A Dominant Pentatonic

C Dominant Pentatonic

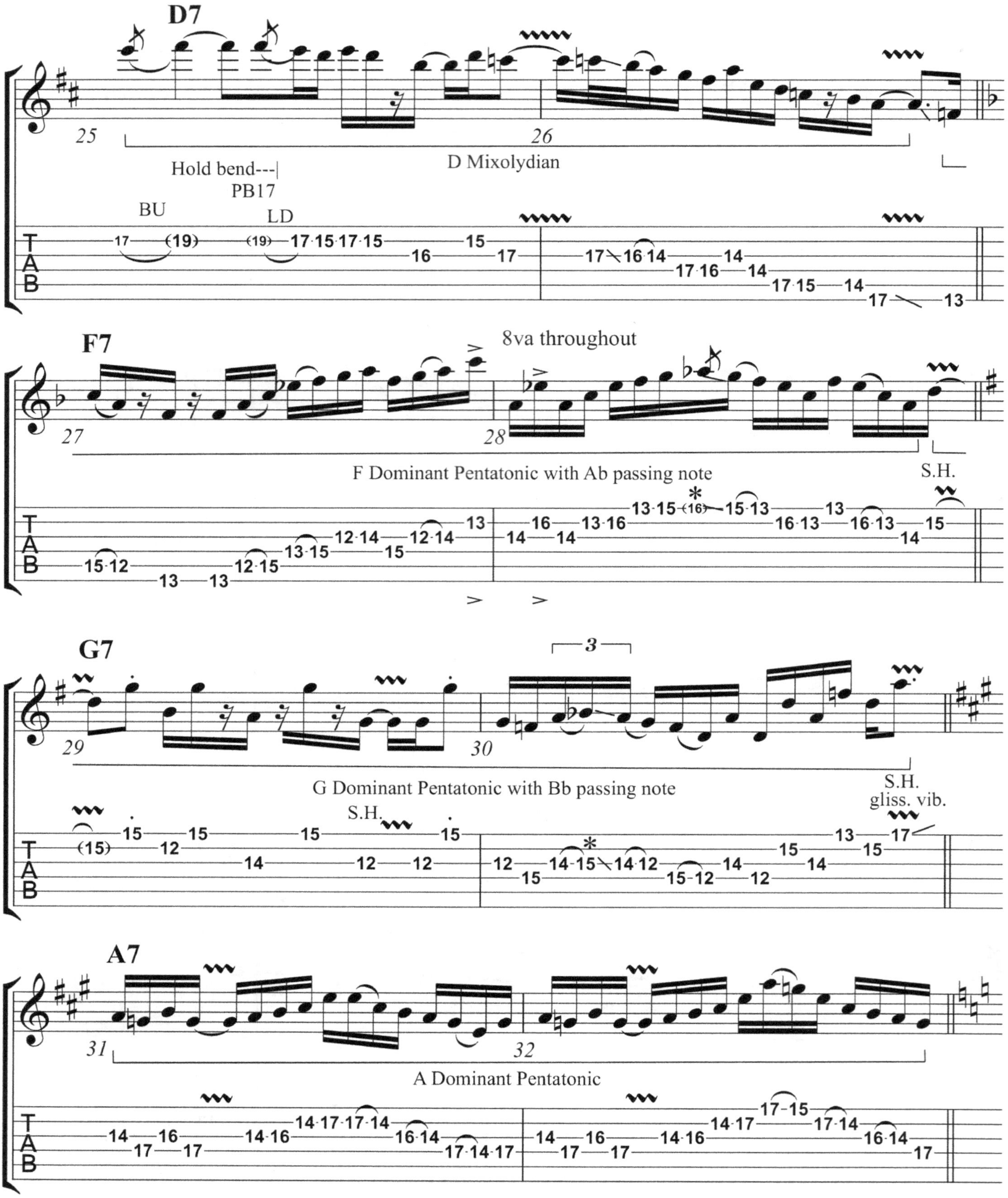
D7
Hold bend---|
PB17
BU
LD
D Mixolydian
F7
8va throughout
F Dominant Pentatonic with Ab passing note
S.H.
G7
G Dominant Pentatonic with Bb passing note
S.H.
S.H.
gliss. vib.
A7
A Dominant Pentatonic

C Dominant Pentatonic

D Dominant Pentatonic

F Dominant Pentatonic

G Dominant Pentatonic

Chapter Eight: Lateral Motion Solo Study

Lateral Motion Solo Study Analysis

This second solo is played over the same A7, C7, D7, F7, G7 chord sequence but is more Funk-Rock in nature.

Because the underlying concept is *lateral motion*, it features several long themes.

Instead of embedding any description regarding modulation in the bar-by-bar analysis, this reference table shows where each technique is applied and you can refer to it as you work your way through the solo.

TRANSITION BETWEEN KEYS	BARS
1) **Semi-tone resolution:** from the old scale to the new one.	The transitions between bars 4-5, 10-11, 26-27, 30-31, 32-33, 36-37
2) **Delayed first phrase in new key:** leave a gap at the start of the new key change.	N/A
3) **Common notes:** join two keys with a note/notes common to both.	The transitions between bars 8-9, 20-21 and 26-27
4) **Anticipation:** play a note early so it is tied over a beat or bar.	End of bars 2 (tied), 12 and 16 (tied rhythm)
5) **Short "pick-up":** played in new key over the last part of the preceding chord/key.	End of bars 4 and 28
6) **Short "pick-up"** played at the end of the previous chord in that key, leading to the new key.	End of bars 32 and 36

Bars 0-2

The solo starts in Shape 3 of the A Dominant Pentatonic. The C natural is just a "vocal" chromatic embellishment that you will be getting used to by now.

Bars 3-4

This section begins in Shape 2 of Mixolydian before shifting down to Shape 1.

The G# chromatic approach note is played as a *grace note* with no significant rhythmic value. It is used to introduce the following A with a slide.

Bars 5-6

These bars contain an adapted version of Example 4f. Here, we've dropped the original line down to a different string-set (D and B strings), transposed it to D, added slides between position shifts, and also modified the ending.

There are four string-skipping ideas in this solo. This first one is based around eight-note groupings and uses various accents to create more expressive interest.

Bars 11-12

The vibrato, although marked on the notation, is quite subtle in this section.

Bars 13-14

Bar thirteen draws from the start of Example 4i, transposed to C and with a modified second half. The wide stretches span over two CAGED shapes simultaneously.

An idea like this may sound fast, but it's no faster than any other section of 1/16th notes. The illusion is created by the fact that the notes jump around a lot in leaps, instead of being played in smaller scale steps.

The second half of bar fourteen features a descending three-notes-per-string C Dominant Pentatonic sequence, which results in diagonal lateral movement. This helps us to escape box-bound playing and it moves down the neck to be better poised to play the following section.

Bars 15-16

Bar fifteen features Example 4d transposed to D, transferred to another string-set, and given a modified ending.

Bars 17-18

As in the first few bars, this section uses some more traditional two-notes-per-string vertical forms of the Dominant Pentatonic (Shapes 3 and 1).

Bars 21-22

The initial ten-note grouping from this section (featuring quite a wide stretch with the fretting hand) contains all five notes of A Dominant Pentatonic compressed into the space of just one string pair. This grouping is then repeated an octave higher on the G and B strings, although the shape must be adapted due to the tuning inconsistency between these strings, and is no longer identical to the first shape.

Bars 23-24

This section begins with a modified version of Example 4m, here transposed to C. It begins with more string-skips and wide stretches and combines lateral motion in bar twenty-three with vertical motion in bar twenty-four (mainly in Shape 4).

Bars 27-28

In bar twenty-eight, the E natural chromatic passing note bridges between F and Eb.

Bars 29-30

The eleven-note groupings in this section feature the kind of three-octave symmetrical relationship of bars 21-22, and represent a rhythmically-displaced version of the eleven-note motif featured in Example 3l.

Bars 31-32

The final string-skipping idea within the solo is Example 4j with a modified ending. It features odd note-groupings and wide stretches with the fretting hand. These elements combine to create an ear-catching, modern-sounding effect. On the recording, I added vibrato to the last note in bar thirty-two using the whammy bar, but you can add it with the fretting hand if your guitar isn't fitted with a bar.

Bars 33-34

Octaves are an effective way of moving laterally on the guitar and provide a symmetrical fingering if you remain on the same strings. In this section, each bar is split into five three-note groupings. As this only produces fifteen of the sixteen 1/16th notes per bar, there is one extra note played at the end of each one.

Bars 35-36

There are two chromatic passing notes used in this section. The first (G#) is used as a bridging note between A and G natural in bar thirty-five. The second (F) is used in the same way as the C natural in bar two.

Bars 37-38

This section features vertical playing from beat 2 of bar thirty-seven. In this case, based on Shape 4 of F Dominant Pentatonic

Bars 39-41

This section uses bar one of Example 4c, transposed to G and with a modified ending.

The clashing semi-tone double-stops provide a grinding vibration that contrasts well with the single notes that lead into them. The final note in bar forty-one is the major third of A7, a strong chord tone.

Exercise

Finally, as an exercise, look back through the solo study making notes in the table below of examples of the various contrasting elements (which will often be juxtaposed within the solo) on the checklist.

MUSICAL ELEMENTS	BARS
Attack: legato vs picking	
Articulation: plain notes vs ones with vibrato, bends, slides.	
Dynamics: notes of even volume vs syncopated accents.	
Rhythms: straight subdivisions vs syncopated ones.	
Note Placement: straight notes vs tied and/or dotted notes.	
Range: low notes vs high ones.	
Melodic contrast: close intervals vs wide intervals.	
Phrase-length: short vs long.	
Texture: single-notes vs double-stops.	
Note duration: long notes vs staccato ones.	
Note density: space vs lots of notes.	

Lateral Motion Solo Study

(S.H. = semi-harmonic   P.H. = pinched harmonic)

(Shaun Baxter)

A7

A Dominant Pentatonic with C natural passing note

C7

C Mixolydian

D7

D Dominant Pentatonic

F7

F Mixolydian

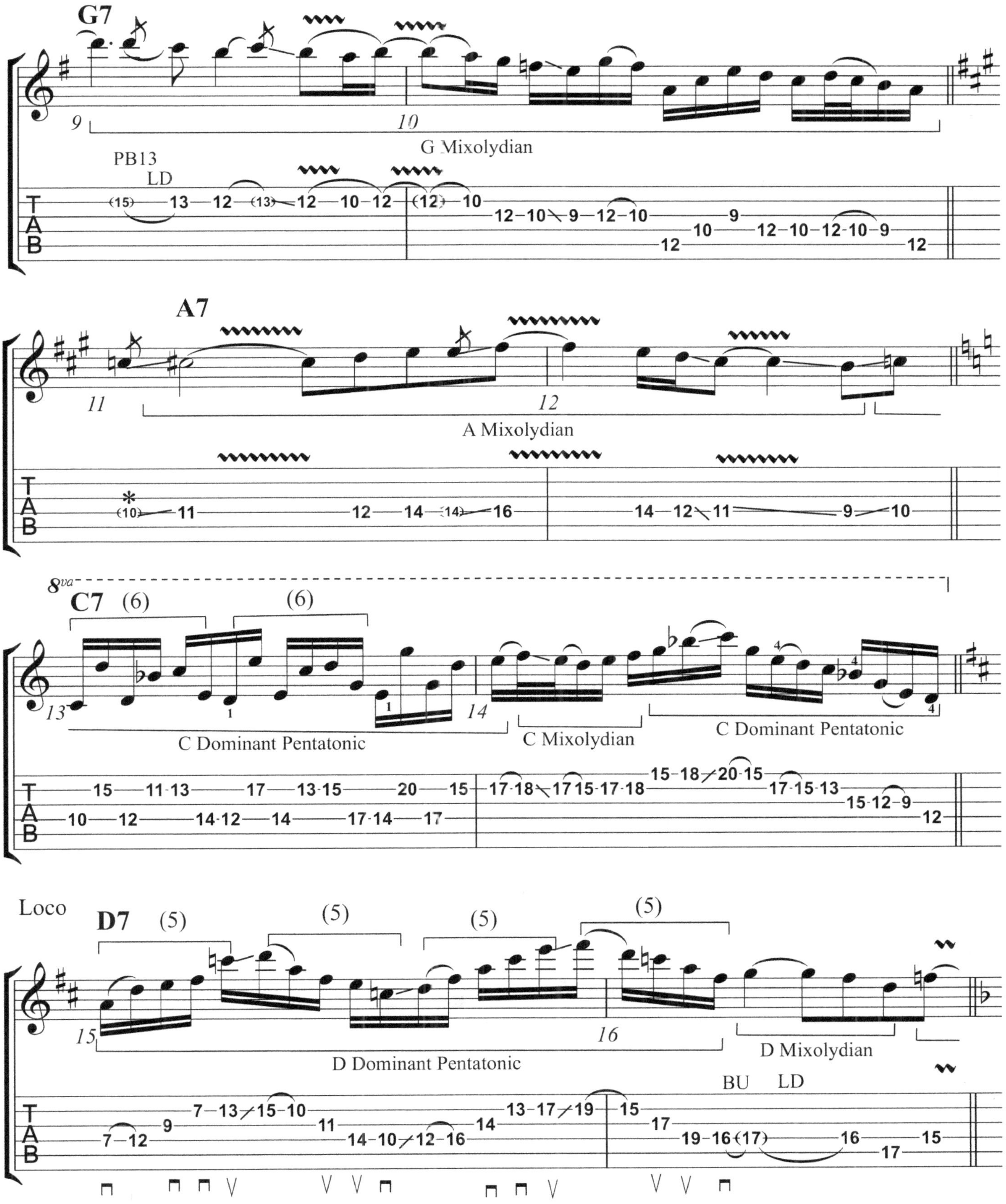
G7
G Mixolydian
PB13
LD
A7
A Mixolydian
8va
C7
(6)
(6)
C Dominant Pentatonic
C Mixolydian
C Dominant Pentatonic
Loco
D7
(5)
(5)
(5)
(5)
D Dominant Pentatonic
D Mixolydian
BU
LD

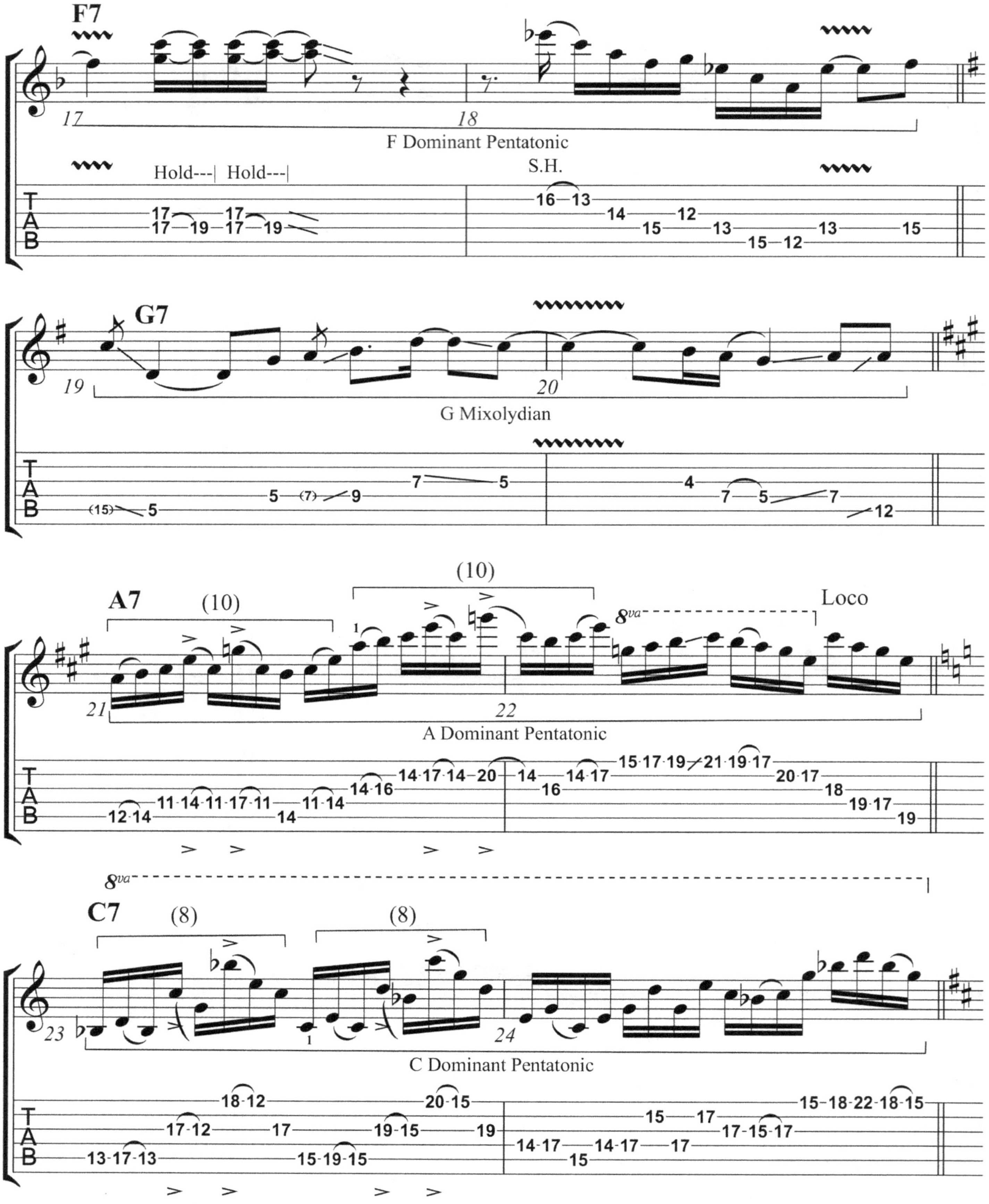
F7
F Dominant Pentatonic
Hold---| Hold---|
S.H.
G7
G Mixolydian
A7
(10)
(10)
8va
Loco
A Dominant Pentatonic
8va
C7
(8)
(8)
C Dominant Pentatonic

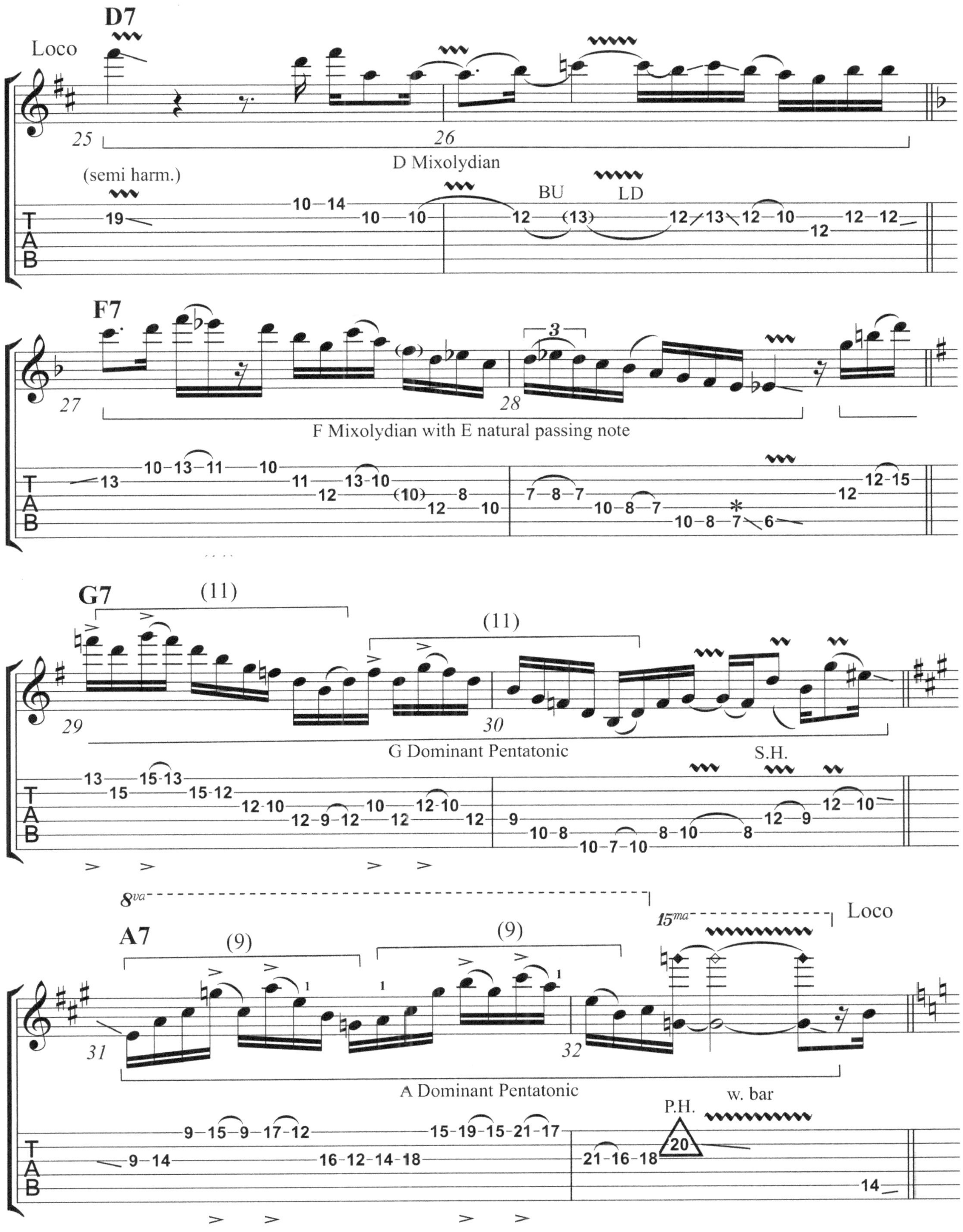

D7
Loco
(semi harm.)
D Mixolydian
BU
LD
F7
F Mixolydian with E natural passing note
G7
(11)
(11)
G Dominant Pentatonic
S.H.
8va
A7
(9)
(9)
15ma
Loco
A Dominant Pentatonic
P.H.
w. bar

C7
C Dominant Pentatonic
Hold
D7
D Mixolydian with G# and F ♮ passing notes
S.H.
BU
LD
F7
F Mixolydian
F Dominant Pentatonic
P.M
P.M.
G7
G Dominant Pentatonic
G Mixolydian
Hold
A7

Chapter Nine: Fast Sequences Solo Study

This solo study demonstrates some different ways of using fast sequences with each of the five shapes of the Dominant Pentatonic, and is based around the following chord progression:

G Dominant Pentatonic   F Dominant Pentatonic

G7 / / /	/ / / /	/ / / /	/ / / /	F7 / / /	/ / / /	/ / / /	/ / / /

A Dominant Pentatonic   F# Dominant Pentatonic

A7 / / /	/ / / /	/ / / /	/ / / /	F#7 / / /	/ / / /	/ / / /	/ / / /

Here are the notes of the F# Dominant Pentatonic scale:

F# Dominant Pentatonic	F#	G#	A#	C#	E
Formula	1	2	3	5	b7

Fast Sequences Solo Study Analysis

Unlike the previous two solo studies, this solo is undiluted Dominant Pentatonic all the way. It is more of a technical workout and certainly wasn't improvised. You can use more legato than is written (for example, in bars 11-12), but ensure that your timekeeping and note clarity is solid.

Bar 0-1

The study begins with a twisted version of a typical Minor Pentatonic lick using Shape 1 of G Dominant Pentatonic. There are no semi-tones in the Dominant Pentatonic, but this lick shows how it is possible to bend up to any scale note from a semi-tone below.

Bars 3-4

Bar three is a straightforward demonstration of how to use Shape 3 of G Dominant Pentatonic. The end of bar four features a pick-up line in Shape 1 of G Dominant Pentatonic, which leads to the key change in the following bar.

Bars 5-6

These bars contain an example of lateral motion using various shapes of F Dominant Pentatonic. Bar five starts with an idea that begins in Shape 2 then shifts up to Shape 3. This same idea continues up the neck, so that in the second half of bar five it begins in Shape 4 and ends in Shape 5. The sequence concludes in the first half of bar six by starting the idea in Shape 1 before finishing in Shape 2.

Bars 7-8

Bar seven demonstrates a range of approaches and shows the scale being played four-notes-per-string (straddling Shapes 1, 2 and 3).

In bar eight, the four-notes-per-string principle is shifted down the neck. This will help with your note visualisation, as it requires you to see several scale shape territories at the same time.

Bars 9-10

Some players might play this A Dominant Pentatonic string skipping idea using hybrid picking but I just used the pick throughout.

Bars 11-12

There are more lateral shifts here in bar eleven. When playing this sextuplet motif, try to visualise the scale shapes, as it occupies the upper reaches of Shapes 3, 4, 5 and 1 of A Dominant Pentatonic in turn.

Most of the runs in bar twelve are in Shape 1 of A Dominant Pentatonic.

Bars 13-15

This section marks the final scale change to F# Dominant Pentatonic and features the longest lateral sequence in the solo.

Remember to visualise the various scale shapes as you shift up the neck.

Bars 16-17

This final F# Dominant Pentatonic Shape 3 melody is played in unison with a keyboard harmony part.

Fast Sequences Solo Study

(Shaun Baxter)

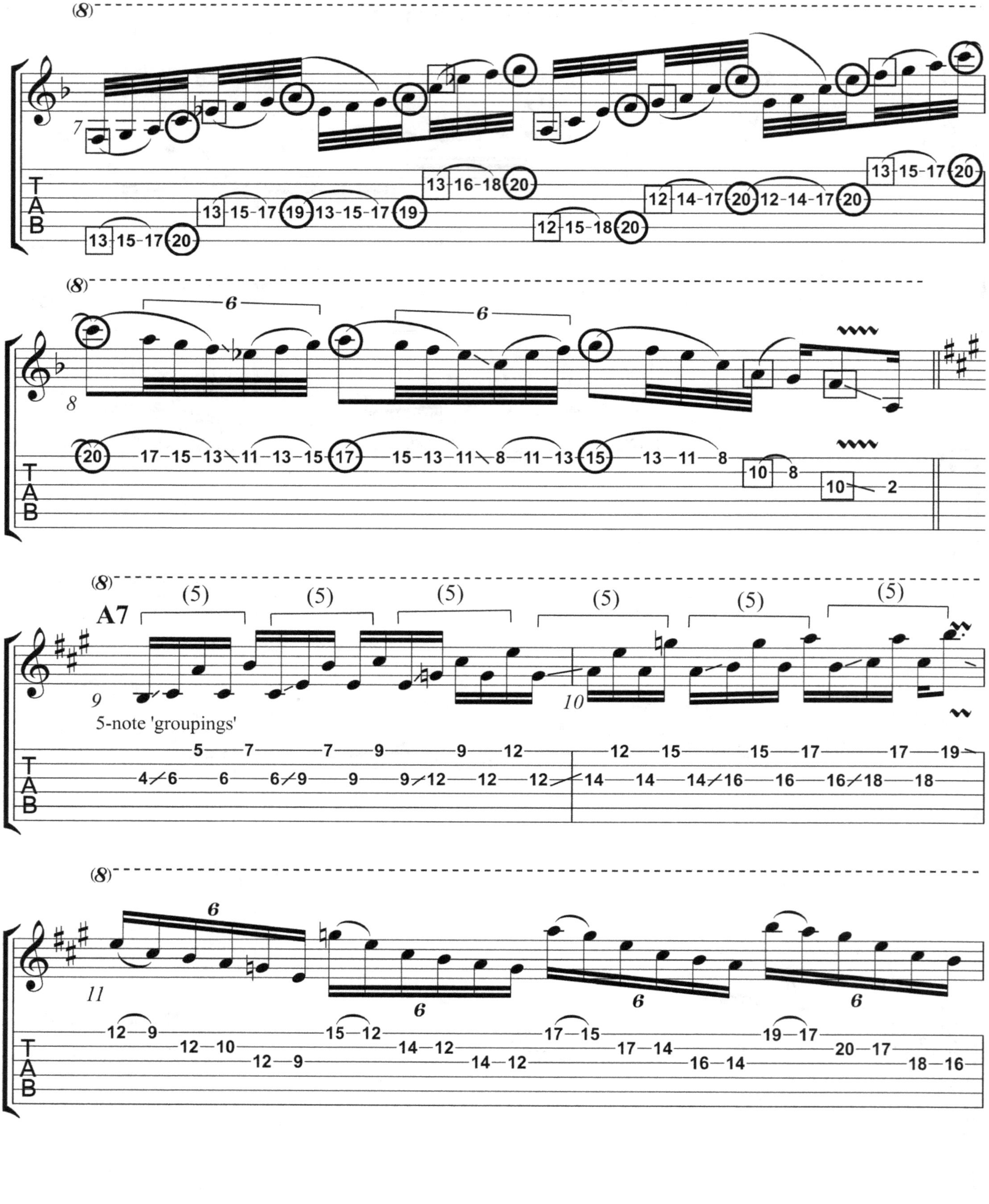
A7
5-note 'groupings'

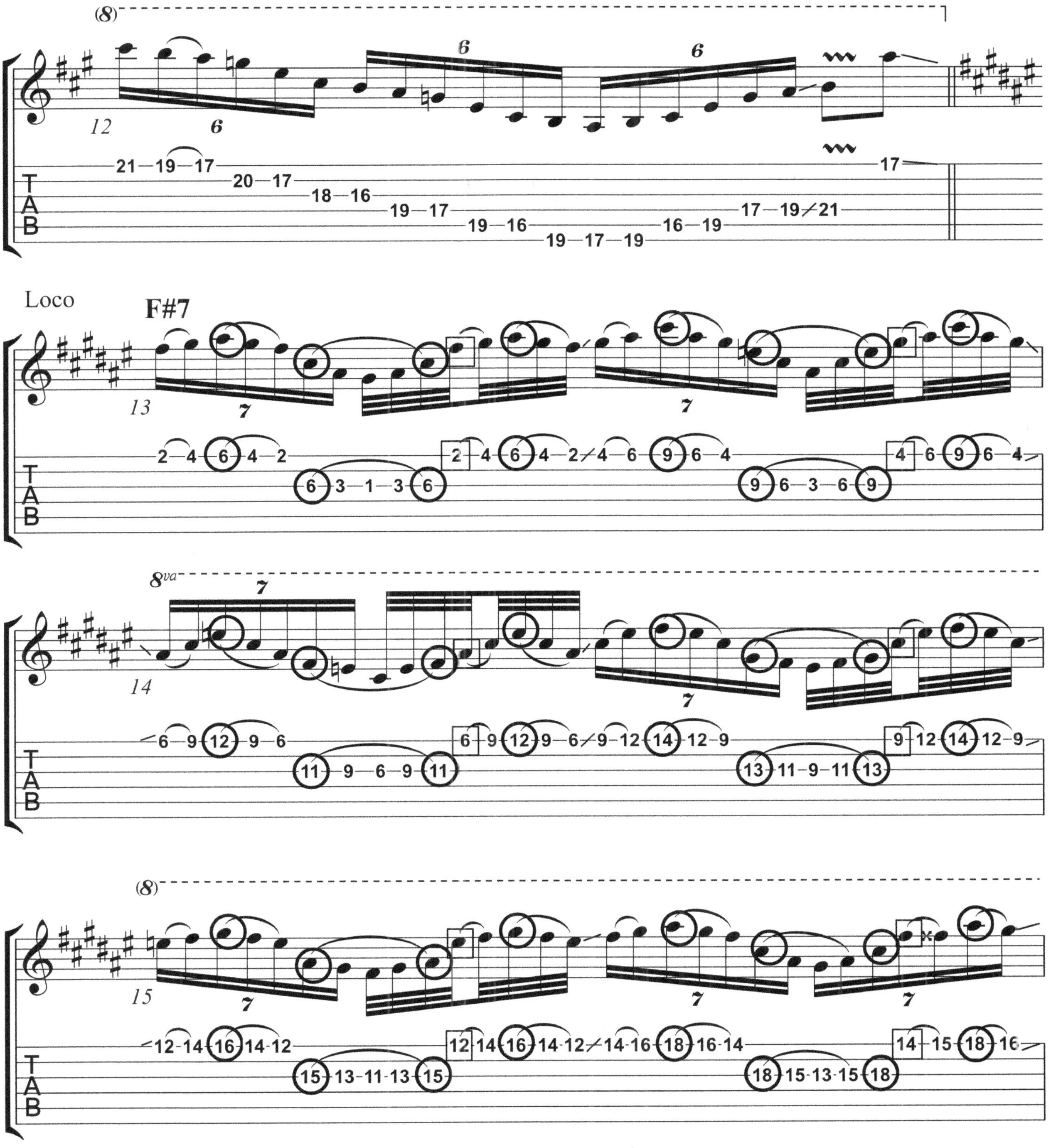
(8)
Loco
F#7
8va
(8)

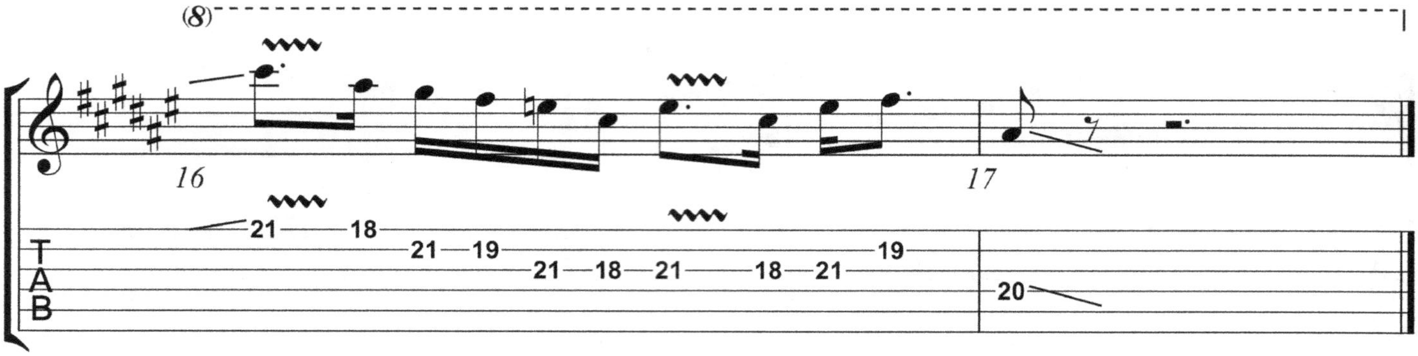
(8)
16
17
TAB
21 18 21 19 21 18 21 18 21 19
20

Conclusion

Now you've worked through all the material in this book, you should be well-acquainted with the Dominant Pentatonic scale. The next step is to write and play your own lines, and work on ways to integrate this useful sound into your playing in a more personal way.

Further Practice

Use either backing track from chapter 6/7 to practice transposing each of the CAGED-based lines in chapters 2-5.

Solos

Balance is critical to an edifying listening experience. The checklists in chapters 6-7 may seem contrived, but they deal with factors that guarantee effective results. With practice, you will start to unconsciously consider these contrasting elements as you improvise, juggling them to engage the listener.

I recommend that you record your development. Apart from helping you to produce your own body of work, it also provides the opportunity to objectively and regularly appraise your playing. When you do that, you'll quickly notice issues around intonation, timing, overplaying, repetitive phrasing patterns etc, and be able to work on fixing them.

Further Application

Although we have studied it in a static context over a dominant 7 chord, it is also possible to use the Dominant Pentatonic over other chord-types.

Blues guitarist Robben Ford uses the Dominant Pentatonic up a perfect fourth from the root of minor 7 or static dominant 7 chords. For example, playing D Dominant Pentatonic (D, E, F#, G, A) over an Am7 or A7 chord produces the notes of the A Minor 6 Pentatonic scale.

Am6 pentatonic scale	A	C	D	E	F#
Formula	1	b3	4	5	6

Jazz musicians like John Scofield and Jerry Bergonzi often play the Dominant Pentatonic launched from various intervals of certain chords. Try exploring the following *substitution* ideas:

- From the b6th over minor 7b5 chords.

- From the 4th over minor 7 chords.

- From the b5th and b6th over altered dominant chords.

- From the 2nd over dominant 9#11 and major 7#11 chords.

I'll leave it to you to analyse the implications of applying each of these substitutions over those chord-types.

Happy practicing!

Shaun

Connect with Shaun

Facebook:

https://www.facebook.com/shaun.baxter.musician

Instagram:

https://www.instagram.com/shaunbaxterguitar/

YouTube:

https://www.youtube.com/@shaunbaxterguitarist

Official website:

https://www.shaunbaxter.com